LEON KIRCHNER

INTERLUDE

for Solo Piano

AMP-8022

Associated Music Publishers, Inc.

DISTRIBUTED BY

HAL•LEONARD®
CORPORATION
7777 W. BLUEMOUND RD. P.O. BOX 13819 MILWAUKEE, WI 53213

Interlude was given its premiere performance on November 11, 1989 by Peter Serkin at the 92nd Street Y in New York City.

duration: ca. 6 minutes

for *Peter Serkin*
Interlude

Leon Kirchner

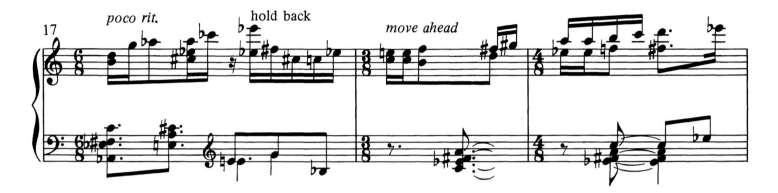

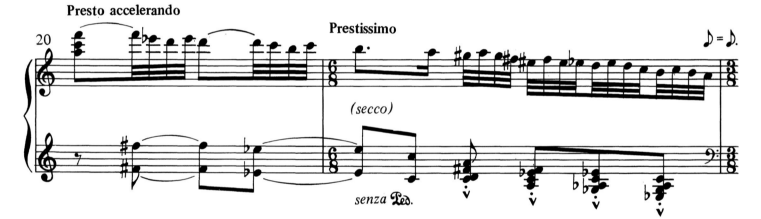

accelerando molto (poco a poco)

♩ = 48

Meno mosso allargando

♩ = 96

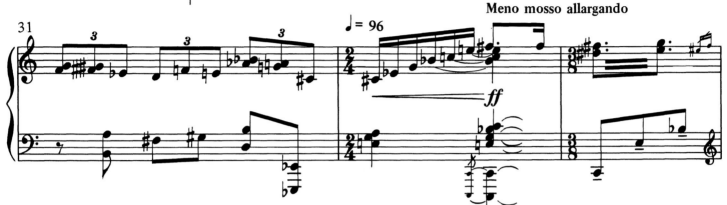

(quasi cadenza)

(tremolos
slow to fast)   ad lib.

G.P.

repeat ad lib.

repeat ad lib.

G.P.
as fast as possible

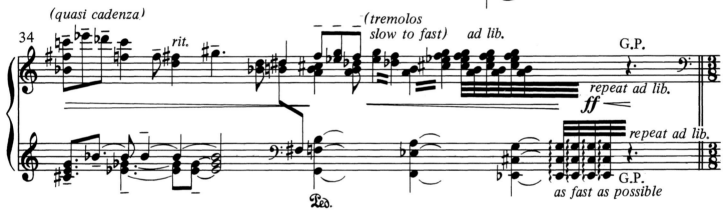

Presto attacca

hold back   accel. al tempo

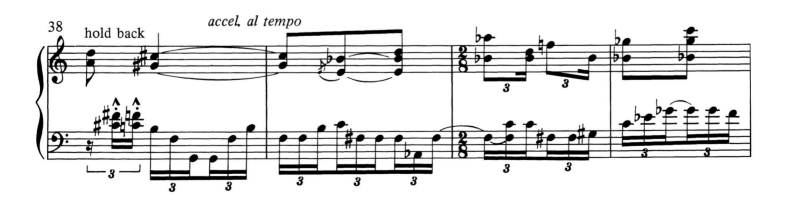

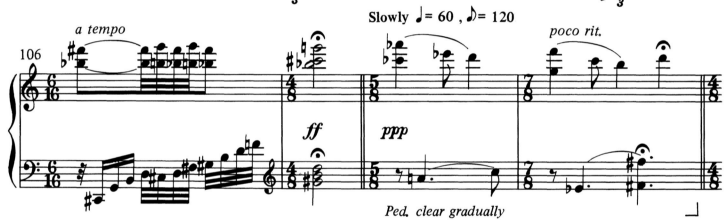

Meno mosso

♪.=♪ poco a poco accelerando = 60 (sometimes faster,

sometimes slower)

♪=♪ (Faster than = 60)

hold back

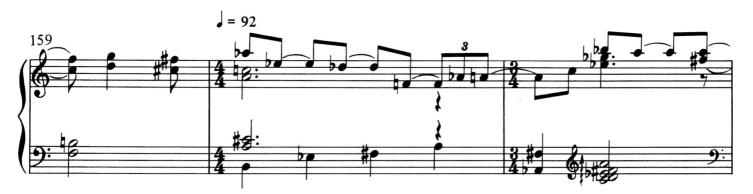

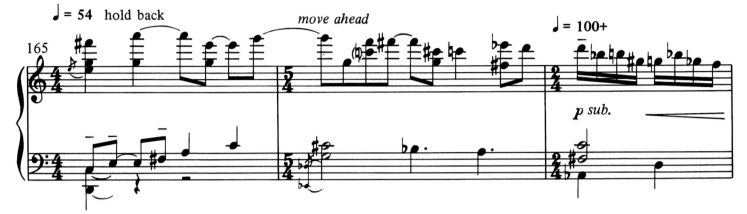

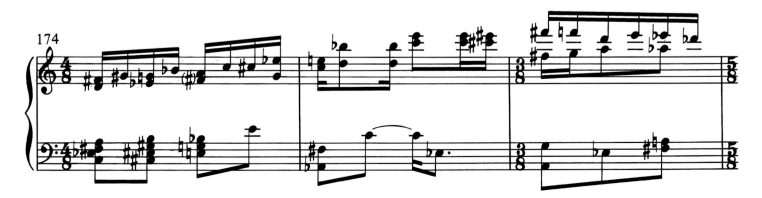

hold back

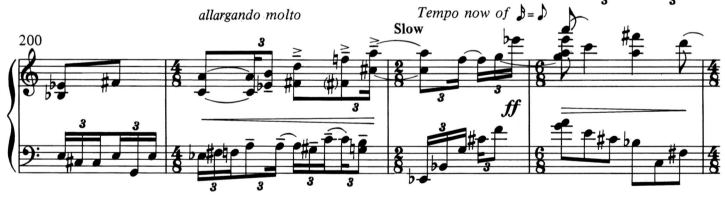

imperceptibly into tremolo